METTĀ

The Philosophy and Practice
of Universal Love

Acharya Buddharakkhita

BUDDHIST PUBLICATION SOCIETY
KANDY   SRI LANKA

Published in 1989

Buddhist Publication Society
P.O. Box 61
54, Sangharaja Mawatha
Kandy, Sri Lanka

ISBN 955-24-0036-8

Typeset at the BPS using an Atari 1040ST
computer and Signum 2.0 software.
Text set in Antique Roman.

Offset in Sri Lanka by
Karunaratne & Sons Ltd.
647, Kularatne Mawatha
Colombo 10

THE WHEEL PUBLICATION NO. 365/366

Contents

Contents

Introduction

The Pali word *mettā* is a multi-significant term
meaning loving-kindness, friendliness, goodwill, be-
nevolence, fellowship, amity, concord, inoffensiveness and non-violence. The Pali commentators define
mettā as the strong wish for the welfare and happiness of others *(parahita-parasukha-kāmanā)*. Essen-
tially *mettā* is an altruistic attitude of love and
friendliness as distinguished from mere amiability
based on self-interest. Through *mettā* one refuses
to be offensive and renounces bitterness, resentment and animosity of every kind, developing instead
a mind of friendliness, accommodativeness and be-
nevolence which seeks the well-being and happiness
of others. True *mettā* is devoid of self-interest. It
evokes within a warm-hearted feeling of fellowship,
sympathy and love, which grows boundless with
practice and overcomes all social, religious, racial,
political and economic barriers. *Mettā* is indeed a
universal, unselfish and all-embracing love.

Mettā makes one a pure font of well-being and
safety for others. Just as a mother gives her own
life to protect her child, so *mettā* only gives and
never wants anything in return. To promote one's
own interest is a primordial motivation of human
nature. When this urge is transformed into the desire
to promote the interest and happiness of others, not

only is the basic urge of self-seeking overcome, but the mind becomes universal by identifying its own interest with the interest of all. By making this change one also promotes one's own well-being in the best possible manner.

Mettā is the protective and immensely patient attitude of a mother who forbears all difficulties for the sake of her child and ever protects it despite its misbehaviour. *Mettā* is also the attitude of a friend who wants to give one the best to further one's well-being. If these qualities of *mettā* are sufficiently cultivated through *mettā-bhāvanā*—the meditation on universal love—the result is the acquisition of a tremendous inner power which preserves, protects and heals both oneself and others.

Apart from its higher implications, today *mettā* is a pragmatic necessity. In a world menaced by all kinds of destructiveness, *mettā* in deed, word and thought is the only constructive means to bring concord, peace and mutual understanding. Indeed, *mettā* is the supreme means, for it forms the fundamental tenet of all the higher religions as well as the basis for all benevolent activities intended to promote human well-being.

The present booklet aims at exploring various facets of *mettā* both in theory and in practice. The examination of the doctrinal and ethical side of *mettā* will proceed through a study of the popular *Karanīya Mettā Sutta*, the Buddha's "Hymn of Universal Love." In connection with this theme we will also look at several other short texts dealing with *mettā*. The explanation of *mettā-bhāvanā*, the meditation on universal love, will give the practical directions for developing this type of contemplation as set forth in the main meditation texts of the Theravada Buddhist tradition, the *Visuddhimagga*, the *Vimuttimagga* and the *Paṭisambhidāmagga*.

1. The Karaṇīya Mettā Sutta

1. Karaṇīyam atthakusalena
    Yan taṁ santaṁ padaṁ abhisamecca
    Sakko ujū ca sūjū ca
    Suvaco c'assa mudu anatimānī

2. Santussako ca subharo ca
    Appakicco ca sallahukavutti
    Santindriyo ca nipako ca
    Appagabbho kulesu ananugiddho

3. Na ca khuddaṁ samācare kiñci
    Yena viññū pare upavadeyyuṁ
    Sukhino vā khemino hontu
    Sabbe sattā bhavantu sukhitattā

4. Ye keci pāṇabhūt'atthi
    Tasā vā thāvarā vā anavasesā
    Dīghā vā ye mahantā vā
    Majjhimā rassakāṇukathūlā

5. Diṭṭhā vā yeva adiṭṭhā
    Ye ca dūre vasanti avidūre
    Bhūtā vā sambhavesī vā
    Sabbe sattā bhavantu sukhitattā

1. Hymn of Universal Love

1. Who seeks to promote his welfare,
    Having glimpsed the state of perfect peace,
    Should be able, honest and upright,
    Gentle in speech, meek and not proud.

2. Contented, he ought to be easy to support,
    Not over-busy, and simple in living.
    Tranquil his senses, let him be prudent,
    And not brazen, nor fawning on families.

3. Also, he must refrain from any action
    That gives the wise reason to reprove him.
    (Then let him cultivate the thought:)
    May all be well and secure,
    May all beings be happy!

4. Whatever living creatures there be,
    Without exception, weak or strong,
    Long, huge or middle-sized,
    Or short, minute or bulky,

5. Whether visible or invisible,
    And those living far or near,
    The born and those seeking birth,
    May all beings be happy!

6. Na paro paraṁ nikubbetha
   Nātimaññetha katthacinaṁ kañci
   Byārosanā paṭighasaññā
   Nāññamaññassa dukkham iccheyya

7. Mātā yathā niyam puttaṁ
   Āyusā ekaputtam anurakkhe
   Evampi sabbabhūtesu
   Mānasam bhāvaye aparimāṇaṁ

8. Mettañ ca sabba-lokasmiṁ
   Mānasam bhāvaye aparimāṇaṁ
   Uddhaṁ adho ca tiriyañca
   Asambādhaṁ averaṁ asapattaṁ

9. Tiṭṭhañ caraṁ nisinno vā
   Sayāno vā yāvat'assa vigatamiddho
   Etaṁ satiṁ adhiṭṭheyya
   Brahmam etaṁ vihāraṁ idhamāhu

10. Diṭṭhiñca anupagamma sīlavā
    Dassanena sampanno
    Kāmesu vineyya gedhaṁ
    Na hi jātu gabbhaseyyaṁ punar etī'ti

6. Let none deceive or decry
   His fellow anywhere;
   Let none wish others harm
   In resentment or in hate.

7. Just as with her own life
   A mother shields from hurt
   Her own son, her only child,
   Let all-embracing thoughts
   For all beings be yours.

8. Cultivate an all-embracing mind of love
   For all throughout the universe,
   In all its height, depth and breadth—
   Love that is untroubled
   And beyond hatred or enmity.

9. As you stand, walk, sit or lie,
   So long as you are awake,
   Pursue this awareness with your might:
   It is deemed the Divine State here.

10. Holding no more to wrong beliefs,
    With virtue and vision of the ultimate,
    And having overcome all sensual desire,
    Never in a womb is one born again.

2. The Background to the Mettā Sutta

The historical background which led the Buddha to expound the *Karaṇīya Mettā Sutta* is explained in the commentary written by Ācariya Buddhaghosa, who received it from an unbroken line of Elders going back to the days of the Buddha himself.

It is told that five hundred monks received instructions from the Buddha in the particular techniques of meditation suitable to their individual temperaments. They then went to the foothills of the Himalayas to spend the four months of the rains' retreat by living a life of withdrawal and intensive meditation. In those days, a month or two before the rains' retreat started, monks from all parts of the country would assemble wherever the Buddha lived in order to receive direct instruction from the Supreme Master. Then they would go back to their monasteries, forest dwellings or hermitages to make a vigorous attempt at spiritual liberation. This was how these five hundred monks went to the Buddha, who was staying at Sāvatthī in Jeta's Grove in the monastery built by Anāthapiṇḍika.

After receiving instructions they went in search of a suitable place, and in the course of their wandering they soon found a beautiful hillock at the foothills of the Himalayas. This, according to the commentary, "appeared like a glittering blue quartz crystal: it was embellished with a cool, dense, green forest grove and a stretch of ground strewn with sand, resembling a pearl net or a silver sheet, and was furnished with a clean spring of cool water." The bhikkhus were captivated by the sight. There were a few villages nearby, and also a small market-town ideal as alms-resort. The monks spent a night in that idyllic grove and the next morning went to the market-town for alms.

The residents there were overjoyed to see the monks, since rarely did a community of monks come to spend the retreat in that part of the Himalayas. These pious devotees fed the monks and begged them to stay on as their guests, promising to build each a hut near the grove on the sandy stretch so that they could spend their days and nights plunged in meditation under the ancient boughs of the majestic trees. The bhikkhus agreed and the devotees of the area soon built little huts in the fringe of the forest and provided each hut with a wooden cot, a stool and pots of water for drinking and washing.

After the monks had settled down contentedly in these huts, each one selected a tree to meditate under, by day and by night. Now it is said that these great trees were inhabited by tree-deities who had a celestial mansion built, appropriately using the trees as the base. These deities, out of reverence for the meditating monks, stood aside with their families. Virtue was revered by all, particularly so by deities, and when the monks sat under the trees, the deities, who were householders, did not like to remain above them. The deities had thought that the monks would remain only for a night or two, and gladly bore the inconvenience. But when day after day passed and the monks still kept occupying the bases of the trees, the deities wondered when they would go away. They were like dispossessed villagers whose houses had been commandeered by the officials of visiting royalty and they kept watching anxiously from a distance, wondering when they would get their houses back.

These dispossessed deities discussed the situation among themselves and decided to frighten the monks away by showing them terrifying objects, by making dreadful noises and by creating a sickening stench. Accordingly, they materialized all these terrifying conditions and afflicted the monks. The monks soon grew pale and could no longer concentrate on their subjects of meditation. As the deities continued to harass them, they lost even their basic mindfulness, and their brains seemed to become smothered by the oppressing visions, noise and stench. When the monks assembled to wait upon the seniormost Elder of the group, each one recounted his experiences. The Elder suggested: "Let us go, brethren, to the Blessed One and place our problem before him. There are two kinds of rains' retreat—the early and the late. Though we will be breaking the early one by leaving this place, we can always take upon ourselves the late one after meeting the Lord." The monks agreed and they set out at once, it is said, without even informing the devotees.

By stages they arrived at Sāvatthī, went to the Blessed One, prostrated at his feet, and related their frightful experiences, pathetically requesting another place. The Buddha, through his supernormal power, scanned the whole of India, but finding no place except the same spot where they could achieve spiritual liberation, told them: "Monks, go back to the same spot! It is only by striving there that you will effect the destruction of inner taints. Fear not! If you want to be free from the harassment caused by the deities, learn this sutta. It will be a theme for meditation as well as a formula for protection *(paritta).*" Then the Master recited the *Karaṇīya Mettā Sutta* — the Hymn of Universal Love—which the monks learned by rote in the presence of the Lord. Then they went back to the same place.

As the monks neared their forest dwellings reciting the *Mettā Sutta,* thinking and meditating on the underlying meaning, the hearts of the deities became so charged with warm feelings of goodwill that they materialized themselves in human form and received the monks with great piety. They took their bowls, conducted them to their rooms, caused water and food to be supplied, and then, resuming their normal form, invited them to occupy the bases of the trees and meditate without any hesitation or fear.

Further, during the three months of the rains' residence, the deities not only looked after the monks in every way but made sure that the place was completely free from any noise. Enjoying perfect silence, by the end of the rainy season all the monks attained to the pinnacle of spiritual perfection. Every one of the five hundred monks had become an Arahat.

Indeed, such is the power intrinsic in the *Mettā Sutta.* Whoever with firm faith will recite the sutta, invoking the protection of the deities and meditating on *mettā*, will not only safeguard himself in every way but will also protect all those around him, and will make spiritual progress that can be actually verified. No harm can ever befall a person who follows the path of *mettā*.

3. Three Aspects of Mettā

The *Mettā Sutta* consists of three parts, each of which focuses on a distinct aspect of *mettā*. The first part (lines 3 to 10) covers that aspect which requires a thorough and systematic application of loving-kindness in one's day-to-day conduct. The second part (lines 11 to 20) expresses loving-kindness as a distinct technique of meditation or culture of mind leading to *samādhi*—higher consciousness induced by absorption. And the third part (lines 21 to 40) underlines a total commitment to the philosophy of universal love and its personal, social and empirical extensions—loving-kindness through all bodily, verbal and mental activities.

Mettā has been identified as that specific factor which "ripens" the accumulated merit *(puñña)* acquired by the ten ways for the acquisition of merit *(dasapuñña-kiriyavatthu),* such as the practice of generosity, virtue, etc. Again, it is *mettā* which brings to maturity the ten exalted spiritual qualities known as "perfections" *(pāramitā).*

The practice of *mettā* thus can be likened to bringing into being a great tree, from the time the seed is sown to the time the tree is heavily laden with luscious fruits and sends forth its sweet odour far and wide, attracting myriads of creatures to it to enjoy its tasty and nutritious bounty. The sprouting of the seed and the growth of the plant are, as it were, brought about by the first part of the sutta. In the second part the tree, robust and developed, is fully covered with fragrant and beautiful flowers, riveting all eyes upon it.

As a pattern of behaviour, the first aspect of *mettā* makes one's life grow like a tree, useful, generous and noble. *Mettā,* as meditation, effects that spiritual efflorescence whereby one's entire life becomes a source of joy for all. The third part envisages in this imagery the fruition of that process of spiritual development whereby one brings about an all-embracing application of spiritual love which can powerfully condition society as a whole and lead one to the heights of transcendental realization.

The human mind is like a mine holding an inexhaustible storehouse of spiritual power and insight. This immense inner potential of merit can be fully exploited only by the practice of *mettā*, as is clear from the description of *mettā* as that "maturing force" which ripens the dormant merits. In the *Mangala Sutta* it is said that only after one has effected an elevating interpersonal relationship (by resorting to good company, etc.) does one choose the right environment for the merits of the past to find fruition. This finding of fruition is exactly what *mettā* does. Mere avoidance of wrong company and living in a cultured environment is not enough; the mind must be cultivated by *mettā*. Hence the allusion to the fruition of past merit.

4. The Ethics of Mettā

Ethics, in the Buddhist context, is right conduct, which brings happiness and peace of mind, and never gives rise to remorse, worry or restlessness of mind. This is the immediate psychological benefit. Right conduct also leads to a happy rebirth, enabling an aspirant to progress further on the onward path to spiritual liberation. It is also the basis for progress in Dhamma here and now. In other words, right speech, right action and right livelihood of the Buddha's Noble Eightfold Path constitute right conduct in the best sense.

Buddhist ethics is twofold: fulfilment of certain virtues *(cāritta)*, and precepts of abstinence *(vāritta)*. *Cāritta*, as found in the *Mettā Sutta,* is as follows:

> [He] Should be able, honest and upright,
> Gentle in speech, meek and not proud.
> Contented, he ought to be easy to support,
> Not over-busy, and simple in living.
> Tranquil his senses, let him be prudent,
> And not brazen, nor fawning on families.

Vāritta is covered by the next gāthā:

> Also, he must refrain from any action
> That gives the wise reason to reprove him.

Cāritta and *vāritta* are thus practised through *mettā* expressed in bodily and verbal action; the

15

resultant inner happiness and altruistic urge is reflected by the aspirant's *mettā* of mental action, as found in the conclusion of the stanza:

> May all be well and secure,
> May all beings be happy!

The ethics of *mettā* thus provides not only subjective well-being, or the opportunity to progress in Dhamma here and now and to enjoy a happy rebirth in the future, but it means the giving of fearlessness and security—*abhayadāna* and *khemadāna*.

An analysis of the behaviour-pattern and traits commended by the *Mettā Sutta* for meaningful interaction, both with reference to persons individually and to society as a whole, provides ample insight into the great implications of the sutta for mental health.

Ability is not just mere efficiency or skill, but means doing a thing well, out of consideration for others, so that one may not cause inconvenience to others. As an able man can become very conceited, the practitioner is advised to be "honest and upright," while being "gentle in speech, meek and not proud"—indeed a perfect synthesis and an equilibrium of traits.

He who is *contented* is "easy to support." Frugality, from consideration of others, is a noble trait. To the extent that one's own needs are cut down as an example to others and as a means not to inconvenience them, to that extent one shows refinement. The more gross and materialistic a person becomes, the more his needs increase. The yardstick to judge the mental health of a given society is thus the diminution of needs, that is to say, the element of satisfaction.

A materialistic and egocentric life is characterized not only by an increase in wants but also by *restlessness*, showing itself in being over-busy and over-active and lacking in moderation and self-restraint. *Mettā,* which promotes the well-being of all, naturally has to be built on such qualities of sober humanism as are reflected in having a few meaningful and select tasks which conduce to the maximum well-being of all concerned.

Living a *simple life* as an expression of *mettā* involves a reorientation of one's outlook and conduct, even in our competitive, pleasure-seeking and possession-minded world. A man of simple living is gentle, yet efficient and effective, and has restraint over his sense-faculties, being moderate, frugal and controlled. Mental culture through meditation for such a person becomes natural and effortless: hence the attribute "tranquil in his senses."

Mettā in conduct includes the exercising of *prudence,* that is to say, practical wisdom. It is only a sagacious and wise person who can really practise *mettā* in all its varied forms in daily life, and through all modes of human relationship. Self-righteousness, arising from a sense of being better or more devout than others, can be (and often is) a masquerade of spiritual practice. To be "not brazen, nor fawning on families" thus is a pointer for the person of *mettā* not to indulge in self-righteousness of any form.

Further, the practitioner of *mettā* is advised *to*

refrain from any action, even social conventions, *for which a wise man may reprove him* as lacking in prudence or propriety. It is not good enough that one should be good, but one should also appear to be good, in consideration not only of one's own well-being but also of others' well-being. An exemplary life is to be lived for the benefit of all, for the welfare of society.

A person living thus now plunges into the cultivation of the all-embracing mind of *mettā* through definite techniques of meditation as envisaged in the remaining part of the sutta.

Mettā is also called a *paritta*—a spiritual formula capable of safeguarding one's well-being, protecting one against all dangers, and rescuing one from mishaps and misfortunes.

When the monks could not stay and meditate in that beautiful forest provided with all facilities because the deities were hostile to them, they had to leave the place. And when they were armed with the protection of the *Mettā Sutta,* which they recited and meditated upon throughout their journey, by the time they reached the place, the deities were full of friendly feelings and already waiting for them. Hostility had been turned into hospitality.

The protection of *paritta* works both subjectively and objectively. Subjectively, as *mettā* cleanses and strengthens the mind, it also awakens the dormant potentials, resulting in the spiritual transmutation of the personality. Transformed by *mettā*, the mind is no longer haunted by greed, hatred, lust, jealousy and those other mind-polluting factors which are one's real enemy and source of misfortune.

Objectively, *mettā* as a thought-force is capable of affecting any mind anywhere, developed or undeveloped. The radiation of *mettā* can not only calm a person or remove the darts of hate from within him, but in some cases can even cure him of severe illness. It is a common experience in Buddhist countries to see how people are cured from all sorts of diseases and freed from misfortunes through the recitation of *paritta*. Thus *mettā* is a real healing power. In this way does *mettā* act as a *paritta,* a healing formula affording safeguards.

5. The Psychology of Mettā

The Pali commentaries explain:

One loves all beings:

(a) by the non-harassment of all beings and thus avoids harassment;

(b) by being inoffensive (to all beings) and thus avoids offensiveness;

(c) by not torturing (all beings) and thus avoids torturing;

(d) by the non-destruction (of all life) and thus avoids destructiveness;

(e) by being non-vexing (to all beings) and thus avoids vexing;

(f) by projecting the thought, "May all beings be friendly and not hostile";

(g) by projecting the thought, "May all beings be happy and not unhappy";

(h) by projecting the thought, "May all beings enjoy well-being and not be distressed."

In these eight ways one loves all beings; therefore, it is called universal love. And since one conceives (within) this quality (of love), it is of the mind. And since this mind is free from all thoughts of ill-will, the aggregate of love, mind and freedom is defined as *universal love leading to freedom of mind.*

From the above passage it will be seen that *mettā*

implies the "outgrowing" of negative traits by actively putting into practice the correlative positive virtues. It is only when one actively practises non-harassment towards all beings that one can outgrow the tendency to harass others. Similarly, it is with the other qualities of inoffensiveness, non-torment-ing, non-destroying and non-vexing in deed, word and thought that one can outgrow the negative traits of being offensive, of tormenting others, of destructiveness and of vexatiousness. Over and above such positive conduct and principled way of life, one further cultivates the mind through that specific technique of meditation called *mettā-bhāvanā,* which generates powerful thoughts of spiritualized love that grow boundless, making consciousness itself infinite and universal.

Thoughts that wish all beings to be friendly and never hostile, happy and never unhappy, to enjoy well-being and never be distressed, imply not only sub-limity and boundlessness, but also utter freedom of mind. Hence the appropriateness of the expression "universal love leading to freedom of mind."

As for the meanings of the five aspects opposed by *mettā, harassment* is the desire to oppress or damage; *offensiveness* is the tendency to hurt or in-jure; *torturing* is a synonym of the sadistic tendency to torment, subjecting others to pain or misery; *destructiveness* is to put an end to or to finish, the trait of the extremist and the iconoclast; *vexing* is to tax, trouble or cause others worry and strain. Each of these tendencies is rooted in antipathy and malevolence, and provides a contrast with *mettā,* both as a mode of conduct and as a psychological state or attitude of mind.

The substitution of a negative trait by the opposed positive course implies a very developed and mature approach to life. The ability to remain non-harassing, inoffensive, non-torturing, non-destructive and non-vexing means a very refined, beautiful and loving mode of behaviour in a world where interaction between human beings creates so much tension and misery.

According to the *Visuddhimagga, mettā* is a "solvent" that "melts" not only one's own psychic pollutants of anger, resentment and offensiveness, but also those of others. Since it takes the approach of friendship, even the hostile one turns into a friend.

Mettā is characterized as that which "promotes welfare." Its function is to "prefer well-being" rather than ill. It manifests as a force that "removes annoyance" and its proximate cause is the tendency to see the good side of things and beings and never the faults. *Mettā* succeeds when it loves, and it fails when it degenerates into worldly affection.

It will be clear from this analysis that only when one tends to see the good in people, and prefers the welfare of others, and accordingly is inoffensive (to remove any annoyance or hurt) and actively promotes well-being, does *mettā* function as a solvent. It is said that the ultimate purpose of *mettā* is to attain transcendental insight, and if that is not possible, it will at least effect a rebirth in the sublime sphere of the Brahma world, apart from bringing inner peace and a healthy state of mind here and now.

Hence the Buddha's assurance in the *Mettā Sutta:*

> Holding no more to wrong beliefs,
> With virtue and vision of the ultimate,
> And having overcome all sensual desire,
> Never in a womb is he born again.

Love wards off ill-will, which is the most damaging of emotions. Hence it is said: "For this is the escape from ill-will, friends, that is to say, the freedom of mind wrought by universal love" (Dīgha Nikāya, III. 234).

In the practice of *mettā* it is important to understand the emotions which nullify *mettā* either by being similar or being dissimilar. The *Visuddimagga* calls them "the two enemies—the near and the remote." Greed, lust, worldly affection, sensuality—all these are said to be the "near enemies" because they are similar in tendencies. The lustful also sees the "good side" or "beauty," and therefore gets involved. Love should be protected from it lest the masquerades of these emotions deceive the meditator.

Ill-will, anger and hatred, being dissimilar emotions, therefore constitute the "remote enemy." The remote enemy can easily be distinguished so one need not be afraid of it, but one should overcome it by projecting a higher force, that of love. But one has to be wary of the near enemy because it creates self-deception, which is the worst thing that can happen to an individual.

It is said that *mettā* begins only when there is zeal in the form of a desire to act. Having commenced through earnest effort, it can be continued only when the five mental hindrances—sensual desire, ill-will, sloth and torpor, restlessness and worry, and doubt—are put down. *Mettā* reaches consummation with the attainment of absorption *(jhāna)*.

6. Meditation on Mettā

There are various ways of practising *mettā-bhāvanā*, the meditation on universal love. Three of the principal methods will be explained here. These instructions, based on canonical and commentarial sources, are intended to explain the practice of *mettā*-meditation in a clear, simple and direct way so that anyone who is earnest about taking up the practice will have no doubts about how to proceed. For full instructions on the theory and practice of *mettā-bhāvanā* the reader is referred to the *Visuddhimagga*, Chapter IX.

METHOD 1

Sit down in a comfortable posture in a quiet place—a shrine room, a quiet room, a park, or any other place providing privacy and silence. Keeping the eyes closed, repeat the word *"mettā"* a few times and mentally conjure up its significance—love as the opposite of hatred, resentment, malevolence, impatience, pride and arrogance, and as a profound feeling of goodwill, sympathy and kindness promoting the happiness and well-being of others.

Now visualize your own face in a happy and radiant mood. Every time you see your face in the mirror, see yourself in a happy mood and put yourself in this mood during meditation. A person in a happy mood cannot become angry or harbour negative thoughts and feelings. Having visualized yourself in a happy frame of mind, now charge yourself with the thought: "May I be free from hostility, free from affliction, free from distress; may I live happily." As you suffuse yourself in this way with the positive thought-force of love, you become like a filled vessel, its contents ready to overflow in all directions.

Next, visualize your meditation teacher, if living; if not, choose some other living teacher or revered person. See him in a happy frame of mind and project the thought: "May my teacher be free from hostility, free from affliction, free from distress; may he live happily."

Then think of other people who are to be revered, and who are also living—monks, teachers, parents and elders, and intensely spread towards each one of them the thought of *mettā* in the manner mentioned already: "May they be free from hostility, free from affliction, free from distress; may they live happily."

The visualization must be clear and the thought-radiation must be "willed" well. If the visualization is hurried or the wishing is performed in a perfunctory or mechanical way, the practice will be of little avail, for then it will be merely an intellectual pastime of *thinking about mettā*. One must clearly understand that *to think about mettā* is one thing, and *to do mettā*, to actively project the will-force of loving-kindness, is quite another.

Note that only a living person is to be visualized, not a dead one. The reason for this is that the dead person, having changed form, will be out of the focus of *mettā*-projection. The object of *mettā* always is a living being, and the thought-force will become ineffective if the object is not alive.

Having radiated thoughts of *mettā* in the order already mentioned—oneself, the meditation teacher and other revered persons—one should now visualize, one by one, one's dear ones beginning with the members of one's family, suffusing each one with abundant rays of loving-kindness. Charity begins at home: if one cannot love one's own people one will not be able to love others.

While spreading *mettā* towards one's own family members, care should be taken to think of a very dear one, like one's husband or wife, at the end of this circle. The reason for this is that the intimacy between husband and wife introduces the element of worldly love which defiles *mettā*. Spiritual love must be the same towards all. Similarly, if one has had a temporary misunderstanding or quarrel with any family member or relative, he or she should be visualized at a later stage to avoid recalling the unpleasant incidents.

Next, one should visualize neutral people, people for whom one has neither like nor dislike, such as one's neighbours, colleagues in one's place of work, bare acquaintances, and so on. Having radiated loving thoughts on everyone in the neutral circle, one should now visualize persons for whom one has dislike, hostility or prejudice, even those with whom one may have had a temporary misunderstanding. As one visualizes disliked persons, to each one must mentally repeat: "I have no hostility towards him/her, may he/she also not have any hostility towards me. May he/she be happy!"

Thus, as one visualizes the persons of the different circles, one "breaks the barrier" caused by likes and dislikes, attachment and hatred. When one is able to regard an enemy without ill-will and with the same amount of goodwill that one has for a very dear friend, *mettā* then acquires a sublime impartiality, elevating the mind upward and outward as if in a spiral movement of ever-widening circles until it becomes all-embracing.

By *visualization* is meant "calling to mind" or visualizing certain objects, such as a person, a certain area or a direction or a category of beings. In other words it means imagining the people towards whom thoughts of love are to be projected or spread. For instance, you imagine your father and visualize his face in a very happy and radiant mood and project the thought towards the visualized image, mentally saying: "May he be happy! May he be free from disease or trouble! May he enjoy good health." You may use any thought which promotes his well-being.

By *radiation* is meant, as explained above, the projection of certain thoughts promoting the well-being of those persons towards whom one's mind is directed. A *mettā*-thought is a powerful thought-force. It can actually effect what has been willed. For wishing well-being is willing and thus is creative action. In fact, all that man has created in different fields is the result of what he has willed, whether it is a city or a hydro-electric project, a rocket going to the moon, a weapon of destruction, or an artistic or literary masterpiece. Radiation of thoughts of *mettā*, too, is the development of a will-power that can effect whatever is willed. It is not a rare experience to see diseases cured or misfortunes warded off, even from a great distance, by the application of the thought-force of *mettā*. But this thought-force has to be generated in a very specific and skilful way, following a certain sequence.

The formula for radiating *mettā* that is used here has come down from the ancient *Paṭisambhidāmagga*: "May they be free from hostility, free from affliction, free from distress; may they live happily" *(averā hontu, abyāpajjhā hontu, anighā hontu, sukhī attānaṁ pariharantu)*. The commentarial explanation of these terms is highly significant. "Free from hostility" *(avera)* means absence of hostility whether aroused on account of oneself or others, or on account of oneself because of others or of others because of oneself or others. One's anger towards oneself might take the form of self-pity, remorse or a gripping sense of guilt. It can be conditioned by interaction with others. Hostility combines anger and enmity. "Free from affliction" *(abyāpajjha)* means absence of pain or physical suffering. "Free from distress" *(anigha)* means the absence of mental suffering, anguish or anxiety, which often follows upon hostility or bodily affliction. It is only when one is free from hostility, affliction and distress that one "lives happily," that is, conducts oneself with ease and happiness. Thus all these terms are interconnected.

By *order* is meant visualizing objects, one after the other, by taking the path of least resistance, in a graduated sequence, which progressively widens the circle and therewith the mind itself. The *Visuddhimagga* is emphatic about this order. According to Ācariya Buddhaghosa, one must start the meditation on *mettā* by visualizing oneself, and thereafter a person for whom one has reverence, then one's dear ones, then neutral people, then hostile persons. As one radiates thoughts of love in this order, the mind breaks all barriers between oneself, a revered one, a dear one, a neutral one and a hostile one. Everyone comes to be looked upon equally with the eye of loving-kindness.

In the *Visuddhimagga* Ācariya Buddhaghosa gives a very apt analogy for the breaking of the barriers: "Suppose bandits were to come to the meditator who is sitting in a place with a respected, a dear, a neutral, and a hostile or wicked person and demand, 'Friend, we want one of you for the purpose of offering human sacrifice.' If the meditator were to think, 'Let him take this one or that one,' he has not broken down the barriers. And even if he were to think, 'Let none of these be taken, but let them take me,' even then he has not broken down the barriers since he seeks his own harm, and *mettā* meditation signifies the well-being of all. But when he does not see the need for anyone to be given to the bandits and impartially projects the thought of love towards all, including the bandits, it is then that he would break down the barriers."

METHOD 2

The first method of practising meditation on *mettā* employs the projection of loving thoughts to specific individuals in order of increasing remoteness from oneself. The second method presents an *impersonal* mode of radiating *mettā* which makes the mind truly all-embracing, as suggested by the Pali term *mettā-cetovimutti,* "the liberation of mind through universal love." The unliberated mind is imprisoned within the walls of egocentricity, greed, hatred, delusion, jealousy and meanness. As long as the mind is in the grip of these defiling and limiting mental factors, for so long it remains insular and fettered. By breaking these bonds, *mettā* liberates the mind, and the liberated mind naturally grows boundless and immeasurable. Just as the earth cannot be rendered "earthless," even so the mind of *mettā* cannot be limited.

After completing the radiation of *mettā* towards selected persons, when the mind breaks the barriers existing between oneself and revered ones, beloved ones, friends, neutral ones and hostile ones, the meditator now embarks on the great voyage of impersonal radiation, even as an ocean-worthy ship voyages through the vast, measureless ocean, nevertheless retaining a route and a goal as well. The technique is as follows.

Imagine the people residing in your house as forming an aggregate, then embrace all of them within your heart, radiating the *mettā* thoughts: "May all those dwelling in this house be free from hostility, free from affliction, free from distress; may they live happily." Having visualized one's own house in this manner, one must now visualize the next house, and all its residents, and then the next house, and the next, and so on, until all the houses in that street are similarly covered by all-embracing loving-kindness. Now the meditator should take up the next street, and the next, until the entire neighbourhood or village is covered. Thereafter extension by extension, direction-wise, should be clearly visualized and spread with *mettā*-rays in abundant measure. In this way the entire town or the city is to be covered; then the district and the entire state should be covered and radiated with thoughts of *mettā*.

Next, one should visualize state after state, starting with one's own state, then the rest of the states in the different directions, the east, south, west and north. Thus one should cover the whole of one's country, geographically visualizing the people of this land regardless of class, race, sect or religion. Think: "May everyone in this great land abide in peace and well-being! May there be no war, no strife, no misfortune, no maladies! Radiant with friendliness and good fortune, with compassion and wisdom, may all those in this great country enjoy peace and plenty."

One should now cover the entire continent, country by country, in the eastern, southern, western and northern directions. Geographically imagining each country and the people therein according to their looks, one should radiate in abundant measure thoughts of *mettā*: "May they be happy! May there be no strife and discord! May goodwill and understanding prevail! May peace be unto all!"

Thereafter one should take up all the continents —Africa, Asia, Australia, Europe, North and South America—visualizing country by country and people by people, covering the entire globe. Imagine yourself at a particular point of the globe and then project powerful rays of *mettā*, enveloping one direction of the globe, then another, then another and so on until the whole globe is flooded and thoroughly enveloped with glowing thoughts of universal love.

One should now project into the vastness of space powerful beams of *mettā* towards all beings living in other realms, first in the four cardinal directions— east, south, west and north—then in the intermediary directions—northeast, southeast, southwest, north- west—and then above and below, covering all the ten directions with abundant and measureless thoughts of universal love.

METHOD 3

According to the cosmology of Buddhism there are numberless world-systems inhabited by infinitely varied categories of beings in different stages of evolution. Our earth is only a speck in our world- system, which again is a minute dot in the universe with its innumerable world-systems. Towards all beings everywhere one should radiate thoughts of boundless love. This is developed in the next method of practice, the *universalization of mettā*.

The universalization of *mettā* is effected in these three specific modes:

1. generalized radiation *(anodhiso-pharaṇā)*,
2. specified radiation *(odhiso-pharaṇā)*,
3. directional radiation *(disā-pharanā)*.

According to the *Paṭisambhidāmagga*, the generalized radiation of *mettā* is practised in five ways, the specified radiation in seven ways, and the directional radiation in ten ways. These ten directional ways may be combined with the five categories of general radiation and with the seven categories of specified radiation, as we will show. In each of these modes of practice, any of the four phrases of the standard *mettā* formula— "May they be be free from hostility, free from affliction, free from distress; may they live happily" —may be used as the thought of radiation. Thus four types of thought applied to five, seven, and 120 objects of *mettā* amount to 528 modes of radiation. Any of these can be used as a vehicle for attaining absorption *(jhāna)* through the technique of *mettā-bhāvanā*. (See Vism. IX, 58.)

Generalized Radiation

The five ways of generalized radiation are as follows:
1. "May all beings *(sabbe sattā)* be free from hostility, free from affliction, free from distress; may they live happily."
2. "May all those that breathe *(sabbe pāṇā)* be free from hostility, free from affliction, free from distress; may they live happily."
3. "May all creatures *(sabbe bhūtā)* be free from hostility, free from affliction, free from distress;

may they live happily."

4. "May all those with individual existence *(sabbe puggalā)* be free from hostility, free from affliction, free from distress; may they live happily."

5. "May all those who are embodied *(sabbe atta-bhāvapariyāpanna)* be free from hostility, free from affliction, free from distress; may they live happily."

Specified Radiation

The seven ways of specified radiation are as follows:

1. "May all females *(sabbā itthiyo)* be free from hostility, free from affliction, free from distress; may they live happily."

2. "May all males *(sabbe purisā)* be free from hostility, free from affliction, free from distress; may they live happily."

3. "May all the Noble Ones *(sabbe ariyā)* be free from hostility, free from affliction, free from distress; may they live happily."

4. "May all worldlings *(sabbe anariyā)* be free from hostility, free from affliction, free from distress; may they live happily."

5. "May all gods *(sabbe devā)* be free from hostility, free from affliction, free from distress; may they live happily."

6. "May all human beings *(sabbe manussā)* be free from hostility, free from affliction, free from distress; may they live happily."

7. "May all those in states of woe *(sabbe vinipā-tikā)* be free from hostility, free from affliction, free from distress; may they live happily."

Directional Radiation

The ten ways of directional radiation involve sending thoughts of *mettā* to all beings in the ten directions. This method, in its basic form, is applied to the class of *beings (sattā)*, the first of the five generalized objects of *mettā*. But it can be developed further by extending *mettā* through each of the five ways of generalized radiation and the seven ways of specified radiation, as we will see.

I. 1. "May all beings in the eastern direction be free from hostility, free from affliction, free from distress; may they live happily."

2. "May all beings in the western direction be free from hostility, free from affliction, free from distress; may they live happily."

3. "May all beings in the northern direction be free from hostility, free from affliction, free from distress; may they live happily."

4. "May all beings in the southern direction be free from hostility, free from affliction, free from distress; may they live happily."

5. "May all beings in the northeastern direction be free from hostility, free from affliction, free from distress; may they live happily."

6. "May all beings in the southwestern direction be free from hostility, free from affliction, free from distress; may they live happily."

7. "May all beings in the northwestern direction be free from hostility, free from affliction, free from distress; may they live happily."

8. "May all beings in the southeastern direction be

free from hostility, free from affliction, free from distress; may they live happily."

9. "May all beings below (in the downward direction) be free from hostility, free from affliction, free from distress; may they live happily."

10. "May all beings above (in the upward direction) be free from hostility, free from affliction, free from distress; may they live happily."

II. 1-10. "May all those that breathe life in the eastern direction ... above be free from hostility, free from affliction, free from distress; may they live happily."

III. 1-10. "May all creatures in the eastern direction ... above be free from hostility, free from affliction, free from distress; may they live happily."

IV. 1-10. "May all those with individual existence in the eastern direction ... above be free from hostility, free from affliction, free from distress; may they live happily."

V. 1-10. "May all those who are embodied in the eastern direction ... above be free from hostility, free from affliction, free from distress; may they live happily."

VI. 1-10. "May all females in the eastern direction ... above be free from hostility, free from affliction, free from distress; may they live happily."

VII. 1-10. "May all males in the eastern direction ... above be free from hostility, free from affliction, free from distress; may they live happily."

VIII. 1-10. "May all Noble Ones in the eastern direction ... above be free from hostility, free from affliction, free from distress; may they live happily."

IX. 1-10. "May all worldlings in the eastern direction ... above be free from hostility, free from affliction, free from distress; may they live happily."

X. 1-10. "May all gods in the eastern direction ... above be free from hostility, free from affliction, free from distress; may they live happily."

XI. 1-10. "May all human beings in the eastern direction ... above be free from hostility, free from affliction, free from distress; may they live happily."

XII. 1-10. "May all those in states of woe in the eastern direction ... above be free from hostility, free from affliction, free from distress; may they live happily."

Explanation

In this technique of universalizing *mettā*, each of the five categories *of generalized radiation* refers to the total dimension of animate, sentient, or organic existence, belonging to the three mundane spheres, namely, the *kāmaloka*, the sphere of sensory existence where desire is the primal motivation; the *rūpaloka*, the realm of the radiant Brahmā gods with subtle form; and the *arūpaloka*, the realm of the formless beings with pure mental life. Whether it is a "being," or that which "breathes," or a "creature," or that which has "individual existence," or that which "is embodied"—all refer to the totality of animate existence, the distinction being that each term expresses comprehensively a certain aspect of life in its entirety.

While visualizing each category one should keep in

mind the specific aspect expressed by its designation. If one trains the mind in the manner of a "mental drill" after having exercised it with the first two methods, the meaning of the five unspecified or generalized terms will become clear. By the time one has completed the two methods, the consciousness will be sufficiently developed and all-embracing. And with such a consciousness, when each of these universal concepts is grasped, the universalization becomes effortless. It may be pointed out that visualization of each of these is no longer of individual objects, but of a concept which is total and all-embracing. The radiation in this case becomes a "flowing out" of love in abundant measure towards the conceptualized mental object—all beings, all creatures, etc.

Each of the seven categories of *specified radiation* comprehends a part of the total range of life, and in combination with the others expresses the whole. *Itthī* refers to the female principle in general, incorporating all females among the devas, human beings, animals, demons, spirits and denizens of hell. *Purisa* means the male principle evident in all the spheres of existence, and both *itthī* and *purisa* together comprehend the entirety. Again, from another angle, the *ariyas* or the spiritually transformed seers, and the *anariyas* or worldlings bound to the wheel of becoming, comprehend the totality. *Ariyas* are those who have entered the transcendental path; they are to be found in the human world and the celestial worlds and therefore they constitute the tip of the pyramid of sentient existence. Worldlings are in all the spheres of existence and constitute the body of the pyramid from the base to the tip, so to say. Likewise, the three categories of *deva, manussa* and *vinipātika* gods, human beings, and those fallen into states of woe—comprehend the totality in terms of cosmological status. *Devas*, the radiant celestial beings, comprise the upper layer, human beings the middle layer, and *vinipātikas* the lower layer of the cosmological mound.

The "mental drill" in terms of *directional radiation,* the radiation of *mettā* to the above twelve categories of beings in the ten directions, makes the universalization of *mettā* a most exhilarating experience. As one mentally places oneself in a particular direction and then lets love flow out and envelop the entire region, one literally transports the mind to the sublimest heights leading to *samādhi*, concentrated absorption of the mind.

When one projects this total wish for others to dwell happily, free from hostility, affliction and distress, not only does one elevate oneself to a level where true happiness prevails, but one sets in motion powerful vibrations conducing to happiness, cooling off enmity, relieving affliction and distress. It will be seen, therefore, that universal love simultaneously infuses well-being and happiness and removes the mental and physical suffering caused by the mental pollutants of hostility, enmity and anger.

7. The Blessings of Mettā

Monks, when universal love leading to liberation of mind is ardently practised, developed, unrelentingly resorted to, used as one's vehicle, made the foundation of one's life, fully established, well consolidated and perfected, then these eleven blessings may be expected. What eleven?

One sleeps happily; one wakes happily; one does not suffer bad dreams; one is dear to human beings; one is dear to non-human beings; the gods protect one; no fire or poison or weapon harms one; one's mind gets quickly concentrated; the expression of one's face is serene; one dies unperturbed; and even if one fails to attain higher states, one will at least reach the state of the Brahma world.

Monks, when universal love leading to liberation of mind is ardently practised, developed, unrelentingly resorted to, used as one's vehicle, made the foundation of one's life, fully established, well consolidated and perfected, then these eleven blessings may be expected.

Anguttara Nikāya, 11:16

Mettā cetovimutti—universal love leading to liberation of mind—signifies the attainment of *samādhi*, absorption based upon meditation on *mettā*. Since *mettā* liberates the mind from the bondage of hatred

41

and anger, selfishness, greed and delusion, it consti-
tutes a state of liberation. Every time one practises
mettā, for however short a period, one enjoys a measure of freedom of mind. Measureless freedom of
mind, however, is to be expected only when *mettā*
is fully developed into *samādhi*.

The various applications of *mettā*, as indicated by
the terms "practised, developed," etc., signify a well-
structured force brought about not only by specific
hours of meditation, but also by converting all one's
deeds, words and thoughts into acts of *mettā*.

By "practised" *(āsevita)* is meant the ardent practice of *mettā*, not as a mere intellectual exercise,
but by committing oneself wholeheartedly to it and
making it life's guiding philosophy, something which
conditions one's attitudes, outlook and conduct.

By "developed" *(bhāvita)* is implied the various
processes of inner culture and mental integration
effected by the practice of meditation on universal
love. Since meditation brings about unification of
mind by integrating the various faculties, it is called
development of mind. The Buddha taught that the
entire mental world is developed by the practice of
meditation on universal love, leading to mind's liberation and the transformation of the personality.

"Unrelentingly resorted to" *(bahulikata)* empha-
sizes repeated practice of *mettā* all through one's
waking hours, in deed, word and thought, and main-
taining the tempo of *mettā*-awareness throughout.
Repeated action means generation of power. All the
five spiritual powers, namely, faith, vigour, mindfulness, concentration and wisdom, are exercised and

cultivated by the repeated practice of *mettā*.

"Used as one's vehicle" *(yānikata)* signifies a "total commitment" to the ideal of *mettā* as the only valid method for the solution of interpersonal problems and as an instrument for spiritual growth. When *mettā* is the only "mode of communication," the only vehicle, life automatically is a "divine abiding" as mentioned in the *Mettā Sutta*.

"Made the foundation of one's life" *(vatthikata)* is making *mettā* the basis of one's existence in all respects. It becomes the chief resort, the haven, the refuge of one's life, making one's refuge in the Dhamma a reality.

"Fully established" *(anuṭṭhita)* refers to a life that is firmly rooted in *mettā*, has anchorage in *mettā* under all circumstances. When *mettā* is effortlessly practised, not even by error does one violate the laws of universal love.

"Well consolidated" *(paricita)* means one is so habituated to *mettā* that one remains effortlessly immersed in it, both in meditation as well as in one's day-to-day conduct.

"Perfected" *(susamāraddha)* indicates a mode of completeness through total adherence and development, leading to that fully integrated state in which one enjoys perfect well-being and spiritual felicity, indicated by the passage detailing the eleven blessings of *mettā*.

The benefits of *mettā* are indeed great and comprehensive. For a follower of the Buddha this is one supreme instrument that can be wielded with advantage everywhere.

8. The Power of Mettā

The subjective benefit of universal love is evident enough. The enjoyment of well-being, good health, peace of mind, radiant features, and the affection and goodwill of all are indeed great blessings of life accruing from the practice of *mettā*-meditation. But what is even more wonderful is the impact which *mettā* has on the environment and on other beings, including animals and devas, as the Pali scriptures and commentaries illustrate with a number of memorable stories.

Once the Buddha was returning from his almsround together with his retinue of monks. As they were nearing the prison, in consideration of a handsome bribe from Devadatta, the Buddha's evil and ambitious cousin, the executioner let loose the fierce elephant Nālāgiri, which was used for the execution of criminals. As the intoxicated elephant rushed towards the Buddha trumpeting fearfully, the Buddha projected powerful thoughts of *mettā* towards it. Venerable Ānanda, the Buddha's attendant, was so deeply concerned about the Buddha's safety that he ran in front of the Buddha to shield him, but the Buddha asked him to stand aside since the projection of love itself was quite sufficient. The impact of the Buddha's *mettā*-radiation was so immediate and overwhelming that by the time the animal neared the Buddha it was completely tamed as though a drunken wretch had suddenly become sober by the magical power of a spell. The tusker, it is said, bowed down in reverence in the way trained elephants do in a circus.

The *Visuddhimagga* records the case of one landlord of Pāṭaliputra (modern Patna), Visākha by name. It seems he had heard that the island of Sri Lanka was a veritable garden of Dhamma with its innumerable shrines and stupas adorning the isle. And blessed with a favourable climate, the people were highly righteous, following the Teaching of the Buddha with great fervour and sincerity.

Visākha decided to visit Sri Lanka and spend the rest of his life there as a monk. Accordingly, he made over his great fortune to his wife and children and left home with a single gold coin. He stopped for some time at the port town of Tāmralipi (modern Tamluk) waiting for a ship, and during that time engaged himself in business and made a thousand gold coins.

Eventually he reached Sri Lanka and went to the capital city of Anurādhapura. There he went to the famous Mahāvihāra and asked the abbot's permission to enter the Sangha. As he was led to the chapter house for the ordination ceremony, the purse containing the thousand gold coins dropped out from under his belt. When asked, "What is it?" he said, "I have a thousand gold coins, sir." When he was told that a monk cannot possess any money, he said, "I don't want to possess it but I wanted to distribute it among all who come for this ceremony." Accordingly he opened his purse and strewed the entire yard of the chapter house, saying, "Let no one who has come to witness Visākha's ordination depart empty-handed."

After spending five years with his teacher, he now decided to go to the famous Cittalapabbata forest, where a good number of monks with supernatural powers lived. Accordingly, he went to the jungle-monastery of Cittalapabbata. On his way he came to a fork in the road and stood wondering which way to turn. Since he had been practising *mettā*-meditation assiduously, he found a certain deva living in the rock there, holding out a hand pointing the road to him. After reaching the Cittalapabbata jungle-monastery, he occupied one of the huts.

Having stayed there for four months, as he was thinking of leaving the next morning, he heard somebody weeping, and when he asked, "Who is that?" the deva living in the manila tree at the end of the walkway said, "Venerable sir, I am Maniliya (i.e. belonging to the manila tree)."

"Why are you weeping?"

"Because you are thinking of going away from here."

"What good does my living here do you?"

"Venerable sir, so long as you live here, the devas and other non-human beings treat each other with kindness. When you are gone, they will again start their wrangling and quarrels."

"Well, if my living here makes all of you live at peace, it is good." And so he stayed on for another four months. It is said that when he again thought of going, again the deity wept. So this Elder stayed on permanently and attained Nibbāna there. Such is the impact of *mettā-bhāvanā* on others, even among invisible beings.

There is also the famous story of the cow. It seems that a cow was giving milk to her calf in a forest. A hunter wanting to kill her flung a spear which, when it struck her body, bounced off like a palm leaf. So mightily powerful is *mettā*—loving-kindness. This is not the case of one who has developed *mettā-samādhi*. It is a simple case of the consciousness of love for the offspring.

Indeed, the power of *mettā* can never be told enough. The commentaries to the Pali Canon are replete with stories, not only of monks, but also of ordinary people who overcame various dangers, including weapons and poison, through the sheer strength of *mettā*—selfless love.

But let not *mettā* be mistaken as a mere sentiment. It is the power of the strong. If the leaders from different walks of life were to give *mettā* a fair trial, no principle or guideline to action would be found to possess greater efficiency or fruitfulness in all spheres.

In everything man is the ultimate unit. If man decides to substitute *mettā* as a policy of action for aggression and ill-will, the world will turn into a veritable abode of peace. For it is only when man shall have peace within himself, and boundless goodwill for others, that peace in the world will become real and enduring.

About the Author

Ven. Acharya Buddharakkhita is founder and president of the Maha Bodhi Society in Bangalore, India. In 1956 he was a member of the editorial board of the Sixth Buddhist Synod in Rangoon, which brought out a complete edition of the Pali Canon. Since then he has written numerous books and translations of Buddhist texts, which have been published in many countries. Best known is his classic English rendering of the Dhammapada, published by the BPS under the title *The Dhammapada: The Buddha's Path of Wisdom.* He also edits and publishes a monthly magazine, *Dhamma.*

An internationally recognized meditation master, he has lived and taught abroad, and founded the Buddhayoga Meditation Society in the United States. He has also taught Buddhology at the Nalanda Pali Postgraduate Institute, Bihar University. Firmly committed to putting Buddhist principles into practice, he has achieved distinction for multi-faceted humanitarian activities in his native India.

BUDDHIST DICTIONARY

Manual of Buddhist Terms
and Doctrines

Nyanatiloka Thera

Since its first publication in 1952, *Buddhist Dictionary* has been a trusted companion and helper in the study of Buddhist literature. The author, the well-known German scholar-monk Nyanatiloka Thera (1879-1957), was qualified as few others have ever been to serve as a reliable guide through the field of Buddhist terminology and doctrine. This book offers authentic and lucid explanations of Buddhist Pali terms, with cross-references in English and source references as well. Amidst the welter of modern books on Buddhism, and translations differing one from the other, this book will help in identifying the doctrinal terms and in correcting misleading renderings. Not a mere word dictionary but an aid to the terminology of Theravada Buddhism, *Buddhist Diectionary* will be as helpful to the serious lay student as to the professional scholar.

265 pages
Hardback

ISBN 955-24-0019-8
Price as in latest catalog

LAST DAYS OF THE BUDDHA

The Mahā Parinibbāna Sutta

The Mahā Parinibbāna Sutta is the Pali Canon's account of the final events in the life of the Buddha. Beginning on Vultures' Peak near the royal capital of Rajagaha, the narrative follows him on his last stirring journey to the small jungle township where he was to attain his final passing away.

During his long ministry the Buddha had taught all that was necessary to reach the goal. In this last phase of his life his primary concern was to impress on his disciples the need to put those same teachings into practice. By his inspiring sermons and serene composure in meeting his end, the Buddha offers the highest possible testimony to his teaching.

This new BPS edition has been freshly revised to improve readability and includes helpful explanatory notes.

120 pages   *ISBN 955-24-0006-6*
Softback   *Price as in latest catalog*

THE BUDDHIST PUBLICATION SOCIETY

is an approved charity dedicated to making known the Teaching of the Buddha, which has a vital message for people of all creeds.

Founded in 1958, the BPS has published a wide variety of books and booklets covering a great range of topics. Its publications include accurate annotated translations of the Buddha's discourses, standard reference works, as well as original contemporary expositions of Buddhist thought and practice. These works present Buddhism as it truly is—a dynamic force which has influenced receptive minds for the past 2500 years and is still as relevant today as it was when it first arose.

A full list of our publications will be sent free of charge upon request. Write to:

The Hony. Secretary
BUDDHIST PUBLICATION SOCIETY
P.O. Box 61
54, Sangharaja Mawatha
Kandy   Sri Lanka